The Twelve Brothers

J. Regina Blackwell

Illustrations by Steve A. Prince – One Fish Studios, LLC

KISSED PUBLICATIONS

Copyright © 2014 J. Regina Blackwell

Published by:
Kissed Publications
P. O. Box 9819
Hampton, VA 23670
www.kplapublishing.com

All rights reserved. Written permission must be secured from the author and/or publisher to use or reproduce any part of this book, except for brief quotations in reviews or articles.

ISBN: 0-9667609-2-1
ISBN-13: 978-0-9667609-2-7
LCCN: 2016933583

DEDICATION

To Mama and Daddy, who found this story; to Karen, who remembers it to this day; to Talitha and Rachael, who inspired me to write this version.

ACKNOWLEDGMENTS

I would like to thank The Brothers Grimm, whose stories have enchanted (and frightened) me since I was a child; my big brothers, Elliotte and Allen, who read them to me; my mother and father, who moved us in walking distance from a library when my sister and I were little, and let my brothers bring lots and lots of books home; my daughters, Talitha and Rachael, who needed me to write this version of the story; my friend Christina Jones-Villa, who read MY "colored" version of "The Twelve Brothers" to her little boy, although both of them are white; my publisher and muse, Kimberly T. Matthews, who wanted to publish this thang and wouldn't let go; my friend, artist Steve A. Prince, who wanted to illustrate Talitha's story; and the One Living God, without Whom I can do nothing.

I love you all forever.

THE TWELVE BROTHERS

Once upon a time, in a happy, green and gold country of beautiful brown people, lived wise, kind King Abdu[1] and Queen Rukiya[2], who had eleven sons. Each of the sons, in addition to being strong and handsome, was adept and skilled in at least one discipline: science, mathematics, music, architecture, finance, art, astronomy, agriculture, history, poetry, or religion. But all, Chinelo, Akil, Liu, Nizam, Fadil, Chijioke, Masomakali, Harith, Tabari, Jawhar, and Shawki[3], were, like their parents, wise in many matters and kind to every living being.

One day the royal family began a great celebration because the royal physician, Moyo[4], had discovered that Queen Rukiya was expecting a twelfth child. But Rukiya was filled with disappointment when her physician told her, a few months before she was due to bring forth the new child, that it would be another boy.

"I love my sons, but I had so been hoping for a daughter this time—to keep me company," she confided to her husband the king. "I watch you with our young men, teaching them to

hunt, to be strong, to be real men —and I envy your connection. The things you have in common."

Abdu smiled and shook his head. "Some of our sons have more in common with you than with me. Jawhar, for example—"

"I mean," the queen interrupted, "I want someone I can teach *woman things*. To pass on the knowledge my foremothers have given me."

"Well, my heart, I suppose I can understand your disappointment," replied the king, "but I am glad you're having another son. After all, a daughter could never gain us a kingdom. She could only lose one." It may have been her pregnancy affecting her, but the queen suddenly felt misunderstood –and a little insulted.

"Is that all you can think of? What your children can *get* for you?"

"My dear!" began the king, but the queen had stormed out of his presence. She ran into the royal suite and snatched off her royal robes before a waiting woman could help her. At first, Rukiya was so angry she noticed no one in the room with her, but as the other women kept touching her, trying to help her, she impatiently commanded them to leave her. Then she pulled out some traveling clothes --her husband's shirts because she was too filled out with child to fit her own. After dressing hastily, and throwing together a few other things in a bag, she seized a pre-nuptial gift --a large, beautiful violet in an ornate earthen pot— and left the castle. No one had the nerve to stop her.

In the middle of a nearby forest, Queen Rukiya dropped, out of breath and sobbing, to her knees. She reached for the violets she had brought with her and placed them next to her knees. Then she began to dig a shallow hole in the rich, black earth. As she dug, she prayed: "Righteous Father, You know I am not ungrateful for my family. I dearly love my husband and my sons, but if –if You could –if You would. . . . I promise to raise her to be righteous as You are righteous, if You would just give me a strong daughter. And, please, if You would also knit her brothers' hearts to her, I would praise You forever." At first, Rukiya thought, amused, *Isn't this a bit much to ask Him?* Then she remembered: *He's God! He can do what He pleases.* So she continued, " Oh, Father, I would that You would be pleased to grant my prayer, and that the answer to my prayer bring glory to Your great name." As she transplanted the violet from the pot to the ground, a lock of her hair fell into the black earth. Rukiya began to weep again. Her tears watered the violet.

In four months, Queen Rukiya brought forth her twelfth son, whom she and the king christened Adisa[5]. (The little boy turned out to be as bright as his brothers, and manifested a propensity for languages.) And twenty-five months later, the queen was found to be with her thirteenth child.

The thirteenth prenatal celebration in the Great Hall of the Palace had roared on for about seven days, with ecstatic dancing, loud music, and the most savory foods, when the royal seer, Enobakhare[6], clothed from neck to toe in a stark white caftan, rose up in the midst of the revelers and cried out in an eerie, high voice:

> *The birth of a thirteenth child*
> *May not be cause for joy*
> *Unless Queen Rukiya's child*
> *Is born a thirteenth boy.*
> *A woman child will bring*
> *Sorrow upon the head*
> *Of princes, queen and king;*
> *Heed well what I have said."*

This announcement, of course, abruptly ended the celebration. Queen Rukiya, who was four months pregnant then and moody as a matter of course, burst into tears and ran from the Great Room to lock herself into the Royal Bedroom. None of her favorite handmaidens could comfort her, and once she emerged from her seclusion, even the King was powerless to do more than quiet her weeping. After the seer's portentous announcement, no one could find Enobakhare to ask for details or clarity. Misery covered Queen Rukiya's face for four months.

For five months, the twelve princes, having understood that the birth of a sister would somehow endanger their lives in particular, decided to live just outside the palace in a great, dark forest. They had agreed upon a signal with their father concerning the birth of the baby: they were to watch the parapet of the palace at the end of the five months for the appearance of a flag. If the flag was green, it meant that the Queen had brought forth another son, and the twelve could return in peace; but if the flag was white, it meant that the Queen had brought a daughter into the world, and the twelve sons should flee for their lives, never to return home.

At the end of five months, the twelve watched the parapet every day for three days, holding their breaths. On the fourth day, a white flag appeared, and the twelve strong and handsome princes left their royal home sadly, believing they would never see it again.

In the palace, although there was great mourning, King Abdu and Queen Rukiya could not help but love their thirteenth child at first sight of her, because the baby princess was so beautiful. Her skin was the color of smooth mahogany; she already had a full head of thick, soft, onyx black hair; her eyes were a wise, sparkly brown; her nose was a round button; her mouth was full and chocolate rose; she was plump and joyful, and even her voice, like a little bell, was a blessing to the ear. The princess seldom cried, and remained alert for long periods of time, apparently examining her new world with clarity. She had a tiny, deep chocolate star between her thick, black eyebrows. The princess' parents did not know what kind of person she would be, so they named her what they could see she was: a "little girl," Talitha.

As the years passed and the King and Queen mourned the disappearance of their sons, yet they rejoiced at every appearance of their maturing daughter, for rather than being evil, as they had feared, the Princess Talitha was, instead, good and powerful, kind and wise, as her parents and brothers had always been. In time, the Princess studied and excelled in each of the twelve disciplines her brothers had mastered. And in time, the King and Queen's greatest sorrow was in the fact that Princess Talitha's brothers would never know and delight in their sister.

Until Princess Talitha reached the age of eighteen years, she never knew she had brothers. Every member of the royal household had been sworn to secrecy. But early one day, while wandering through the green and gold halls of the palace, she came upon a room she had never seen before. Finding the door locked, the princess hesitated only a moment before removing two slender but ornate, heavy hair pins from her braided thick hair, and gently manipulating them in the lock until she heard the tumblers fall. The princess turned the copper doorknob and entered the room.

The room's walls were papered in green and gold; the room itself was full of clothing — beautiful men's clothing: silk shirts, linen trousers, satin stoles, soft leather shoes, belts and boots, pure virgin wool jackets, pants of soft cotton—and all dyed in the most wondrous blood reds, jungle greens, earthy browns, ebon blacks, rich gold, and, of course, royal purples. Princess Talitha cried out like a baby with the pleasure of looking at and touching the dazzling array of clothing, hung carefully in twelve recesses along the walls of the room.

"Whose clothes are these?" she asked herself aloud. She knew they weren't her father's — not all of them; many were too small or too young in design for her old, stuffy father the King. She had just noticed that a different monogram decorated all of the clothes in each recess when she heard a soft step behind her. Princess Talitha turned.

"These are the clothes of your twelve brothers, my princess," spoke the seer Enobakhare, enveloped in dead white. And the prophet told the princess her life story. By the end of the story (when the beautiful princess picks the lock of the mysterious door), Princess Talitha was sitting on the lush green carpeted floor, not feeling so powerful as she usually did.

"But what evil will I wreak upon them?"

"Who can tell, Princess?"

"Surely I can control my own will. I am not evil hearted. And true evil can only be deliberately, intentionally wrought, can it not?"

"Who can tell, Princess?"

"*You* can tell, Seer," replied the princess, finally standing in irritation. "You can tell me *something*. *You will* tell me something." The "or else" hung in the air, unsaid, but not unheard.

"Yea, Princess, I can tell this: the question is not 'what evil can you do?' but 'what evil can you *un*do?'" And before the princess could open her mouth, the Seer had turned and departed. (Enobakhare alone, among all King Abdu and Queen Rukiya's subjects, could leave the royal presence without permission.)

The princess angrily rushed out to find her parents. When she did find them (her father was watching her mother clip roses in the royal garden), she exploded.

"How could you let me live without knowing?" was all she said at first, but the King and Queen exchanged a look of complete, sorrowful understanding. "Surely," continued the princess, "you could have told me about my brothers. They know about me!"

"We would have told you," began the King slowly, "had the circumstances been different. As it was —. "

"You were afraid I'd seek them out and harm them!" the princess gasped.

"No, daughter. We only feared to burden you with a ridiculous guilt."

"'Ridiculous'?" echoed the princess.

"Yes," spoke the Queen for the first time. "Fate so often seems ridiculous."

"'Fate'?" The princess fell silent, thinking, *This is what separates me from my brothers: a ridiculous fate.* "Tell me about them," she finally said.

King Abdu and Queen Rukiya were surprised at the delight that rushed up within them at the princess' demand. It was as if the desire to boast about their twelve wonderful sons had lain enchanted, asleep, for eighteen years, and could not have been awakened save by that one voice speaking those four words.

So the King and the Queen and the Princess sat on the ground in the garden, and the parents told stories about their twelve sons to the thirteenth child. Often interrupting each other, stumbling over their own and each other's words, and even speaking some words in unison, Abdu and Rukiya told the happy stories, the sad stories, the funny stories, the frightening stories, the strange stories, the important stories, and the unimportant stories about their twelve sons. They told stories that illustrated the personalities, skills, weaknesses, habits, and needs of their twelve sons. They told stories about the friends, enemies, loves and acquaintances of their twelve sons. They told stories that other people, family, advisors, servants, onlookers, had told of their twelve sons. By the time Abdu and Rukiya stopped telling stories, the moon had risen and was beginning to fade again before the dawn; their voices were ragged and hoarse, their cheeks blotted with falling, dried and fresh tears.

And Talitha had wept, too. Finally she asked the question she had asked the day before: "How could you let me live without knowing?" And one other question: "How could you live without telling me?" Yet even as she asked these questions, she knew there was no answer — none the King and Queen could give her, in any case. *A ridiculous fate,* she kept thinking, *separates me from my twelve fine brothers.*

For three days and nights, the princess neither spoke nor slept after that. The servants and advisors to the royal family, wisely sensing great agony of soul, whispered and tiptoed about.

But Enobakhare the seer was nowhere to be found.

At supper, the King and Queen met each other's eyes over the Princess' weary head with apprehension. Outside, a storm, complete with gray, brooding clouds, over the palace threatened, and there seemed to be a storm threatening within the walls as well.

At the beginning of the fourth day, the storm broke with a great clash of thunder. It was the same clash that heralded Princess Talitha's entrance into Enobakhare the Seer's solitary, drafty, brightly lit suite of rooms, located in a parapet of the palace. The Seer turned from a great old book on a stone table to meet the burning eyes of Princess Talitha.

"Where are they?" she demanded.

When the King and Queen learned of their daughter's firm intention to bring her brothers home, they were filled with dismay. But neither of them resisted Princess Talitha's resolve.

"We have attempted to thwart Fate," murmured Rukiya. "But although it was a grand struggle, we remain powerless." The King folded his wife into his arms.

"There is still hope," he said. "We will continue to pray."

In that hope, the royal city saw Princess Talitha off with great rejoicing. There were three days of singing, dancing and eating, the last of which Talitha enjoyed with gusto: who knew when she would next eat so well?

On her journey, the princess would carry three changes of light-textured, dark green clothing, most of which were coveralls with cowls or hoods; seven changes of undergarments; a black cloak; she carried insect-repelling salves and healing ointments; strong, but light-footed brown boots; a sharp, short heavy knife in a thick, leather sheath, a heavy bag (which converted into a enveloping sleep pallet) made of leather and canvas, to carry over one shoulder; a stout walking stick (which doubled as a sort of bayonet when its shoe was removed); several short, thick rolls of white cotton cloth; a brown loaf of soy bread as big and round ("and as hard," said the King) as Talitha's head; and a skin of water. The food would last several weeks if the princess ate and drank sparingly. The princess left her golden crown and gorgeous robes at home.

Early in the morning of the fourth day, Princess Talitha bound up her braided hair and set off in search of her brothers. She began her journey trudging through the great, dark forest, the edge of which her brothers had inhabited months before her birth. The forest was so great, she had been told, that it would take two months to cross it on foot, even if it hadn't been filled with strangling snakes, slavering wolves, smothering sand pits, sharp-toothed panthers, poisonous plants and seemingly starving, ever-present insects. Talitha learned quickly never to lean, stand, sit or lie on any thing before careful examination.

But the forest was beautiful, too. Filled with multitudinous shades of green life and gold light, clear pools dancing with silver fish, riotous (in sound and appearance) birds, and the most marvelous insects, the forest became a delight as well as a challenge to the princess. She soon learned to spear the fish that moved, as well as looked, like mercury, and found that a book knowledge of plants and animals (acquired in eighteen years of palace schooling) would save her life a thousand times.

Her favorite creatures were spiders, some of which were hardy enough to catch small fish in their waterproof webs. The princess admired spiders most because of their tenacity: the willingness to fashion and re-fashion webs, whether the originals were destroyed by prize or peril; the patience to wait and wait for the thrill of a thread, which betokened survival; and the boldness ready to fight any enemy, regardless of size. Ants were as bold, but lacked separate wills, individuality. Bees had the same mindless drive as ants. No, spiders were best, displaying initiative, creativity, courage, and (most easy for the princess to immediately identify with) the ability to cope with prolonged solitude.

Her solitude broke on the third week of Princess Talitha's trek. While sitting on a (carefully examined) rock just long enough to wipe her brow and take one swallow of water from her bag, the princess heard the snap of a twig, the whisper of leaves against cloth and the jingle of a bell. Having dashed quickly, quietly, carefully behind a broad, ivy draped tree, the princess stared in the direction of the sounds. Her heart thudded in her ears. One of her twelve brothers?

No, for though he was a man, and apparently of royal birth, he carried no green and gold. His family's colors were, apparently, black and gold, for that was what he, and the night-black horse he was leading, wore. His feet were covered in dull black hunting boots, his well-muscled legs, slim gold trousers; he wore a matching light, gold jacket with a cowl which was black on one side and gold on the other. There was a square on his right breast pocket that was cut into four smaller squares, one gold, one black, one black, one gold. He was much taller than Talitha (who stood taller than the tallest woman in her kingdom); he had beautiful broad shoulders, and his biceps bulged in his sleeves. *A pretty shape!* thought the princess. *Curse that cowl for covering his face!* The sound of bells came from the horse's braided leather harness, which was also black and gold, as was the saddle and the blanket under the saddle.

"Whoever you are," said suddenly a deliciously deep voice from the cowl, making the princess jump, "it's too late to hide. I have seen you already. Come out. I mean you no harm." As the speaker was coming closer with each word and obviously headed straight for her hiding place, Talitha quickly, quietly unsheathed her short knife (though she did not hold it out in the open) and stepped out from behind the tree.

"'Harmless' hardly hides," said Talitha, gesturing with her free hand at the cowl. The stranger, understanding, removed his cowl, revealing deep ebon brown skin, deep set brown eyes, a wide-nostriled nose, full lips, and crisply thick, black, close-cropped hair. He smiled, disclosing perfect teeth and a dimple in his chin, but it was too late for the dimple: the stark planes along his cheeks had already snared Talitha's heart.

"I was hardly the one hiding," he responded. "My name is Prince Kamau[7]. But my mother," he went on, "called me Abayomi[8]." He paused. "I don't tell many people that name. Are you in trouble?"

"I am Talitha. I come from the kingdom far on the other side of this forest. I am not in trouble, but I am far from home, seeking twelve lost kinsmen."

"Are *they* lost, or are *you*?" Kamau smiled again. "My kingdom is far on that side of the great forest, six weeks away, but you are welcome to ride home with me and restore your provisions." He patted his horse's neck, and it snorted and shook its head. "Montsho[9] can bear the weight of another friend." Kamau's eyes twinkled as he added, "You see I call you 'friend' – although your knife has not yet decided." Talitha's face grew hot as she brought the knife out from the folds of her cloak and sheathed it.

"Your offer is kind to a stranger, but I cannot forsake my quest. It may not last much longer, and after I find my brothers, we can seek out your kingdom, so that you may celebrate with us."

"Your brothers? They do not live in the kingdom? Or," Kamau quickly added, as a shadow fell over Talitha's face, "Maybe they are on a hunting trip, as I am."

"I will tell you the story one day, should my quest be successful," Talitha said simply.

"Well, if I cannot persuade you to come home with me," responded the prince, "maybe you will stop at the cabin yonder. It's not mine, to offer its hospitality, but the young woodsman who lives there seems friendly enough. Allow Montsho and me to show you the way. Would you like to ride? " Talitha inclined her head at this fresh kindness, although she refused the ride, so Prince Kamau also walked, alongside his horse, holding the rein, as he led Talitha to a little cabin in the forest. It was so craftily built to be hidden among the shadows and trees of the forest that, had Talitha not met the prince, she might not have found the cabin alone.

"Hello, the house!" cried Kamau as the two approached. The door opened, and Talitha looked into the face of her youngest brother. She knew it was he by his stark resemblance to her mother. He was the same height as Talitha, broader across the shoulders, but carried his mother in his smooth, heavy eyebrows, long, dark eyes, and sculptured lips. His skin was the color of carob powder. Before she knew it, Talitha had flung herself at him, startling Kamau and the young man both.

"God be praised, brother! I am your sister, Talitha," she explained once she had caught her breath. "Look at me. Can't you see I am your kinswoman?" As Adisa held the stranger at arm's length, he could. The mixed feelings of bitterness and fear that he and his brothers had known for eighteen years gave way to wonder as Adisa gazed upon the lovely, open face of his sister.

"There is my father," Adisa whispered, "in the shape of your brow and the line of your nose. But," he continued, as tears flowed from his eyes, "your smile is my mother's." Adisa realized then that he had no choice but to love his sister, regardless of fate or prophecy. He knew his brothers would feel the same.

"It appears there *will* be a celebration," murmured Kamau. He could feel his eyes burning, too.

"Yes!" replied Adisa. "The celebration starts now. Please stay with us, Kamau, until my eleven brothers return, and share our joy."

"My desire is here," said Kamau, as his eyes gently brushed Talitha's face, "but I have been away from home for more than a month now. I must return to the kingdom. However, at the palace, I will make ready to receive you and your brothers, to continue the celebration." Talitha turned to Kamau and embraced him, too.

"Surely I, with your mother, can now call you Abayomi. Providence brought us together," she said.

"Neither my mother nor my father is with me any longer," responded the prince, "so I haven't heard that name in a long time. I like the sound of it from your lips. I am overjoyed that your quest has come to a happy end. You and your twelve brothers must not forget to bless my kingdom with a visit. Please."

"It will give us great pleasure to share our joy with you, Kamau, our benefactor," said Adisa. The prince climbed upon his black horse and, saluting the reunited brother and sister, rode away.

At nightfall, Talitha's other brothers, Chinelo, Akil, Liu, Nizam, Fadil, Chijioke, Masomakali, Harith, Tabari, Jawhar, and Shawki, returned. (They had been hunting, as Kamau had surmised.) Each was envious that it had not been his turn to stay home that day, and so be the first to welcome their sister after eighteen years. At first sight of her, they, too, loved Talitha with all their hearts. And Talitha found that looking at her brothers was like looking at portraits of her beloved parents.

"Our parents," said Tabari, "must learn of this reunion. As soon as possible, we must all return home and end their worries." All the brothers and Talitha agreed, but Masomakali pointed out, "It will be another whole day before we can be ready. But after that, come the dawn, we must be on our way." So that night, the twelve princes and their princess sister feasted and regaled each other with stories of their lives while they had been apart. They felt so much joy, they could hardly sleep for the excitement at the thought of seeing their parents' faces.

The next morning, Chinelo, Akil, Liu, Nizam, Fadil, Chijioke, Masomakali, Harith, Tabari, Jawhar, Shawki, Adisa, and Talitha began packing up everything portable in the cabin. And then, at one point, all of the princes had to leave Talitha: each of them had left something in the forest that he wanted to take back with him.

"We will return," they said, "cook supper, and begin our rest for the morning's journey." And off they went, in twelve different directions, it seemed.

Alone in the cabin, Talitha decided to decorate the only thing they would not be able to carry home: the large, heavy table Nizam had built for meal times. Talitha went outside the cabin, looking for beautiful plants, and she was charmed to find twelve violets growing together, but alone, in a clearing. Talitha had seen violets in the forest before, but never so many blooms in one plant, and never so large. Each blossom was as large as the palm of Talitha's hand, with royal purple petals surrounding a gold center. Talitha knew such a gorgeous bouquet, as a centerpiece to her brothers' table, would gladden their last day in the cabin.

She sang as she plucked the violets, but as soon as she had gently snapped the stem of the last one, Talitha heard a thunderclap, and the sky darkened about her. She turned at the sound of a soft step behind her, and was hardly surprised to see the face of Enobakhare.

"Good cheer, Seer," she greeted him. "I suppose you have learned of my safe reunion with my brothers." Talitha said these last words almost with gloating, remembering the prophecy with which Enobakhare had troubled their lives.

"'Safe'?" responded the prophet. "But what is that in your hand?"

"They are flowers for my brothers' table," said Talitha, and she was about to add, "Aren't they beautiful?" when she looked again at them and saw that they were very quickly wilting. "Oh, the poor things! I should never have plucked them!"

"You are quite right, Princess," said Enobakhare. "For these are more than flowers: these are the bodies of your twelve brothers, who are now soaring the wind in the shape of ibis. Unless you can undo the harm you have wrought them, they will remain sacred waterfowl forever." By now, Princess Talitha had fallen weakly to her knees in horror. The wilting violets she managed to keep, though, gently cradling them in her hands.

"Dear God!" she whispered. "This is what the prophecy meant. But how can I undo this horrible thing?"

"You must listen carefully, Princess, and fail not to accomplish my every word. From this day forth, you may not speak, or even laugh, until you have fashioned, with your own hands, a needle grass cloak for each of your twelve brothers. Nor can any of you ever return to your parents until you have finished your task. As for these violets, drop them. Let them return to the earth from which they came. When you are able to speak again, they will bloom again." Talitha complied, letting the violets fall to the ground. Immediately, they turned black and sank into the earth. But Talitha had one more question.

"'Needle grass'? I have never heard of such a plant," said the Princess.

"You have lived a happy life thus far," responded the Seer. "Needle grass grows only in graveyards and otherwise barren places. It is a vindictive plant, not at all like violets: it stings and blisters the hand that uproots it." With these words, Enobakhare disappeared as quietly as he had appeared.

Talitha shuddered; still, she determined in her heart to accomplish every word of the seer, lest her brothers remain ibis forever. She remembered the question the Seer had asked her long ago: "What evil can you *undo*?" And from the moment she made that decision, she stopped speaking, spending her days alone, searching for more and more needle grass to make cloaks for her brothers. Her hands became feverish and covered with blisters; still, she spent every waking hour either picking needle grass or sitting in her brothers' cabin, painstakingly fashioning cloaks. Her brothers, now in the form of iridescent black and white ibis, brought her grains and nuts, and occasionally a frog (for which Talitha was grateful, but refused to eat).

Three months after Talitha had begun her new quest, Prince Kamau returned to the forest. "Hello, the house!" he called, as he and Montsho approached the cabin. At the sound of his voice, Talitha dropped the cloak she had just finished and rushed to the door. Kamau ran to embrace her, but was dismayed when the princess fell to her knees and began silently to weep.

"These are not tears of joy, such as we shared when we parted," he said, as he raised the Princess to her feet. "What is the matter? Where are your brothers?" Of course, Talitha could not answer him; she only shook harder with grief, though she was very careful not to make a sound. After a while, she ceased to cling to the Prince, and she went back into the cabin and sat down to begin another cloak. Kamau followed her. "Why are you so silent? Can you not even call me by the name my mother gave me?" he asked, looking into her face. But when Talitha's tears fell afresh, Kamau stopped questioning her and began pacing the floor.

"I came back to find out why you and your brothers had not come to my kingdom for the celebration. I can see now that I am too late, somehow. What is this you are making? Oh, God!" the Prince whispered, at the sight of Talitha's hands. He noticed, too, how thin and ashen she appeared. "What has happened here? I should never have left. All right, you needn't explain anything to me, but you must let me take you home to your family." When Talitha emphatically shook her head, silently weeping again and covering her face with her hands, the prince changed his tactic.

"Then, please, Talitha, if you cannot go home, come home with me. I myself will make certain that you eat, and I will bathe your hands myself. Please, Talitha, if you do not hate me for leaving you, please come with me." The prince's pleas prevailed upon Talitha, and, gathering the few cloaks and all of the needle grass she had into her bag, she climbed upon Montsho, who stood as still as stone while she did so.

"Noble beast!" Kamau praised his horse, watching. "Hold me tight, now," he said to Talitha, as he mounted in front of her. Talitha secured her bag around her waist and then firmly clasped the Prince about his. She sighed and relaxed, resting her cheek on the Prince's back. Kamau clucked to the horse, and Montsho was off home.

The two rode for days, stopping every now and then to dismount, stretch their legs, drink and eat. Some evenings they slept outside — or, at least, Kamau did. Talitha continued to silently seek out needle grass and work on her brothers' cloaks. By this time, Kamau had surreptitiously watched Talitha at this work for a long while, but he had stopped asking questions and had determined not to interfere at all-- except to take her to his home, where he felt she would at least be comfortable. And whenever they came upon running water along the way, Kamau would stop and bathe Talitha's blistered and burning hands. Once, while he was carrying out this kindness, Talitha pulled one hand away and caressed his cheek with the back of her fingers. Kamau did not look up into her face at this, but he caught her hand again, and, before continuing to bathe it, he lightly kissed it. Then he said, "Let's go on." And they rode on until, finally, the two reached Kamau's kingdom.

The sentry on the watchtower of Castle Obsidian saw, afar off, two riders on Prince Kamau's horse and cried the news to another sentry, who took the message inside the castle. By the time Kamau and Talitha had approached the gates, Prince Kamau's uncle, Minkah Chafulumisa[10], was there to meet them. He was a tall, serious-faced man, dressed in gold robes curiously embroidered in glittering black. His skin was the color of loamy earth, and his voice was as deep as a lion's; though he spoke with quiet joy at the sight of Kamau, Minkah was obviously surprised to see his young nephew accompanied by the ashy, poorly-dressed beauty with circles under her eyes.

"Welcome home, nephew--and welcome to your companion . . . uh?" Minkah said, waiting for a name.

"Uncle, this is Princess Talitha," Kamau said, as he helped her dismount. A servant led Montsho away to the stables. "This is the woman I told you about the last time I came home. She has . . . come upon hardship and is in need of succor. I have offered her our home to rest and strengthen herself--for as long as she needs to stay."

THE TWELVE BROTHERS

Minkah nodded in understanding and agreement. "And what is your trouble, Princess? How otherwise can we offer assistance to you?" But before Talitha would refuse to answer, Kamau spoke up, taking Minkah aside: "She would rather not speak of this trouble. And I, too, wish to exercise the utmost discretion. Let us leave her in peace, uncle, as much as we can." Minkah bowed his head in assent.

"Of course," he replied, and then clapping his hands, told waiting servants, "Make ready the best rooms for our guest!" And to Talitha, he said, "You will stay in my rooms, for as long as you like." And whispered to a servant: "Draw a bath for the Princess as well; use plenty of aromatic oils."

Kamau talked to the silent Talitha: "Although we must separate for now, try not to feel like a stranger. To this household-- my household-- you are a kinswoman. As soon as you are rested and refreshed, we will reunite and dine together." Talitha almost smiled at the Prince's words of comfort, and then she allowed the castle's servant women to lead her away to her chambers.

She fell asleep several times in the hot bath full of flower petals, while the women gently massaged her feet and hands – and murmured disapprovingly at the pitiful state of those hands. The eldest servant, called Umm[11], was bold enough to say, "I am sixty years old and my experience tells me, from your bearing, that you are a noble woman, Princess; but if we had to judge you by your poor hands--! What have you been doing?" Umm did not wait for an answer (she seldom did), but, clucking in consternation, ordered medicinal salves for Talitha's hands while the others unbraided, washed, dried and dressed her hair, and then dried, oiled and powdered her skin with the most wonderful smelling ointments and talcs. (They even brushed her teeth and scraped her tongue.) As the women finished dressing Talitha in lovely, soft robes of gold satin, the salves Umm had called for arrived --in the hands of Kamau.

"I couldn't wait for supper," he said, ignoring Umm's dark disapproval, "and since Umm would be scandalized if I bathed you myself" -- Umm scowled while the other women gasped and tittered-- "I settled for bringing the salves myself." This time, Talitha did smile; the luxurious bath and the beautiful robes had done much to restore her. But she did not forget her mission. She knew that she would not sleep that night, but begin again on her brothers' cloaks and the search for more needle grass. Kamau did not understand Talitha's quest, but he showed how well he was beginning to understand her: with the salves, he brought two pairs of gloves, one fingerless pair of soft gold lace, "To wear to dinner," he said; about the other pair, which were lined with down and made of thin, but strong leather, he said nothing. But Talitha knew what he expected them to be used for.

"You women may all leave," he said, "all except Umm, since she will not leave anyway, while I am here."

"Wise prince, you well know that a noble woman needs a female companion at all times when in a strange place," answered Umm. The other women left.

But before the door closed, another woman entered, saying, "And since I'm here, you needn't remain at all, brother. Not that you will pay any of us any mind," she added. The woman offered her hand to Talitha. "I'm Rachael[12], Kamau's sister," she said. She was a shorter, feminine version of Kamau, having a deep, beautiful brown face with high cheekbones and white flashing teeth. Her eyes were slightly lighter than her brother's and her hair longer: it was a thick black halo about her head. "How beautiful but sad you are, Princess! Do not be troubled: Kamau has not betrayed any confidence, and knowing him, he never will. But you may safely tell me nothing, Talitha, because, as you can tell already, I speak my mind. Still, we pray to God for you, to replace your sadness with peace." Rachael gently embraced Talitha and kissed her on the cheek. "And if there is anything I can do to help you--besides pray--you have only to speak."

"But the Princess does not speak much," interposed Umm meaningly.

"Then we will read her wonderful eyes! Or," answered Rachael, gazing at the elder woman suddenly without the merriment, "we will do-- and say -- nothing. That has been known to help, at times, as well." And Umm bowed her head, cowed by Rachael's gaze. Apparently, despite her self-deprecating words, Rachael was also like her brother in understanding and diplomacy. While Rachael talked to Umm and Talitha of inconsequentialities – what to expect for dinner and whether the cooks knew what they were about that night --Kamau gently applied the salve to Talitha's hands, and then gingerly helped her slide the lace gloves on. Talitha's heart turned over again as their eyes met briefly.

I love you, Abayomi, thought Talitha, as she experienced the prince's tender solicitation, *And no wonder, for you are the kindest and noblest of men, besides my brothers and my father. The wonder is that you love me, too: a suddenly, strangely silent and lone woman. What can you know of me, to love me?*

But Kamau would not meet her inquiring gaze again. *I cannot look into those eyes long, Talitha,* he thought. *They are deep pools; even a strong man could lose himself in them. And if I am to help you at all, to love you at all, I cannot lose myself--not yet.*

For Kamau had counted the ibis which had followed Talitha from the forest and now lived near the lake behind Castle Obsidian. He remembered waking during the nights of their trek through the forest, secretly watching Talitha silently fashion cloaks from blistering weeds. Kamau could not tell what evil had bound the thirteen siblings; still, somehow, he understood that Talitha was doing what she could to destroy the yoke of enchantment. Kamau understood that whatever Talitha had to do, she had to do it herself, alone, and that the best way he could help her was to keep others from hindering her. He devoted himself to that work, even, he decided, if he had to leave his kingdom again, with Talitha, until she finished her task.

Supper that night in the Castle's great hall was filled with uncomfortable silences and stilted conversation. Everyone's eyes were drawn to the beautiful, silent girl who ate hardly anything. Minkah looked surreptitiously at the girl. The handmaidens of his niece had braided Talitha's heavy hair into a glistening black crown atop her head. When she lifted her chin, the girl looked regal. Minkah suspected that Kamau had not been duped into accepting a common maid as a princess; it was obvious that the girl had, at least, a great deal of royal blood. *Still, while diplomacy and soft spokenness were virtues where women are concerned, the uncle thought, taciturnity was completely inappropriate! What was the matter with the girl?*

Rachael amused herself with watching her brother watch Talitha, thinking, *The man is lost to us forever!* She was glad that her brother had finally found a woman to his liking, silent and mysterious though she was. Rachael found Talitha lovely, and she was relieved that the princess had not that "delicate" loveliness which had become fashionable lately. Here was obviously a hardy beauty, proof against even the forest. This woman already bore herself as a strong queen should. But Rachael hoped the mystery would dissipate soon. She had little patience with mystery.

Kamau, who knew that Talitha would not speak (though he was not quite sure why), attempted to hide her silence from the company. His attempts fell flat, and they all breathed a sigh of relief when Minkah clapped his hands for the clearing of the table. The men and the women separated (Kamau and Talitha glancing wistfully at each other), and Rachael and Umm took Talitha back to her chambers.

"You look weary, as well as sad and beautiful," said Rachael.

"She kept falling asleep in her bath, Princess," volunteered Umm.

"I've been known to do that myself, after hunting with Kamau," replied Rachael. "In any case, Talitha, you need rest and probably solitude, which can be helpful in times of trouble." When they reached Talitha's chambers, Rachael kissed her again and said, "Rest well, my sister. Perhaps morning will bring an end to trouble. If you need anything, pulling the bell rope near your bed will summon Umm or one of the other servant women." Umm bowed her head and wished Talitha a good night as well.

In another bedroom, Minkah's sleep was troubled and filled with dreams that were trying to remind him of something: a man in white robes speaking over a baby. What had he said?

"A woman child, born with a star,
Will gladly take this man child far:
When she brings him back again,
His reign can never be the same.
Twelve sacred birds will surround this royal house;
They come for the woman, and not her future spouse.
The twelve ibis are more than birds,
But twelve brothers and warriors: hers.
Mark well the woman, the star on her head;
Mark well these words that I have said."

Suddenly, Minkah awoke and sat straight up in bed. The man in white had been prophesying over Kamau's birth. That day, Kamau's father, the king, Minkah's brother, had spoken to Minkah: "We must be vigilant about the women my son encounters." On his deathbed, the king reminded Minkah about that vigilance: "You must promise me, brother, to protect my son from the evil woman." None of the house had ever questioned the idea that the prophecy boded ill. As he remembered the king's dying words, Minkah remembered something about the regal, silent princess. He had seen, between her dark eyebrows, a tiny, deep burnt umber star.

In the darkness of the bedchamber he had temporarily moved into (so that his nephew's guest would be comfortable), Minkah reached for the rope beside his bed and summoned a servant.

Talitha, behind the closed doors of Minkah's bedchamber, did not sleep at all. She needed to finish the cloak she had been working on and find more needle grass. She had been fortunate thus far: the nasty weed was really not that difficult to find, only difficult to work with. Talitha noticed that in her absence, the clothes she had brought with her, her traveling clothes, had been cleaned and folded neatly on Minkah's bed. Talitha slipped out of the gorgeous robes she had been given and into one of her dark green coveralls, pulling the cowl over her braids and forehead. After she had drawn on the leather gloves that Kamau had brought her and a pair of soft soled short boots, Talitha grabbed her sack and quietly, quickly left her chambers, searching for a way out of the castle.

When she finally did get outside and find the royal family cemetery, she thought she had done so unseen. She was wrong. She had fallen upon her knees in a patch of needle grass and was stuffing handfuls into the sack when the whisper of her name made her feel as though she had been snatched inside out. She whirled around to meet Rachael's astonished gaze.

"What in time are you doing?" the young woman asked, and then waved her hand distractedly, as if trying to wipe out her question. "You won't answer that. You don't speak. Let's start over. . . . How can I help you? Can I pick some of those horrible weeds, too?" Talitha quickly threw up both hands to stop Rachael. Then she pulled off one glove, trying to remind Rachael of her own ruined skin. Rachael waved her hand at Talitha again.

"If you can stand it, so can I," she argued. And since she seemed determined to help, no matter the cost, Talitha quickly handed Rachael her sack. "Fine," Kamau's sister responded, as if Talitha had spoken to her. "I'll hold the sack, and you fill it. I guess it really wouldn't do for Uncle to think that your blisters are catching!" Talitha gazed upon her friend with gratitude and tried to embrace her, but Rachael protested. "No, we haven't time for that. We've got to fill this bag quickly and get you back to your room before Umm notices that you--that we—are missing and alerts the whole castle! I told her just to leave *you* alone, and, of course, what *I* do is none of her business, but I doubt Umm will pay me any mind whatsoever!"

So the two women made short work of filling Talitha's sack; then they rushed, as quietly as they could, back to Talitha's room. Rachael pushed Talitha into her room with the sack, saying, "You should come get me the next time you need to go out. It takes less time if you have help. Mmmph! The things I do to get a decent sister-in-law!" And after making this embarrassing comment, Rachael went back to her room to sleep. Talitha stayed awake, working with the stinging needle grass, fashioning them into cloaks, little knowing that someone besides Rachael had seen her at work outside the castle.

Umm went straight to Minkah with her report. The brow of Kamau's uncle turned dark with anger. "So this is what he brings home with him: an evil sorceress to bring to naught all that his forebears have worked for." And Umm saw the great man tremble, but she did not know that it was not with fear of the sorceress. Even before Minkah had had Talitha followed, he had heard reports of the twelve ibis. One servant (though not a prophet) had said the presence of the sacred birds was a sign of blessing upon the royal house of Kamau. But Minkah had realized what the birds actually were. He had recognized what the star on Talitha's forehead meant. He knew he must plan, and quickly.

The next evening, for supper, the waiting women had dressed Talitha in crimson robes--and they had done more. At Minkah's command, they had secretly littered her bath with a sleeping potion, which would affect Talitha before the meal ended. When, to the dismay of everyone (except Minkah), Talitha collapsed at the table, Kamau rose with a cry and ran to her side to cradle her in his arms.

"What has happened?" Kamau turned to his uncle for help. Minkah, who had also risen, spoke solemnly after a practiced pause: "Who can know, Prince? Perhaps it is exhaustion. Perhaps illness. In any case, we should take the princess back to my rooms. I will summon the physicians." While Kamau carried Talitha himself, vainly calling her name, Rachael and Umm followed. Minkah stayed behind, to summon and advise the royal physicians.

Minkah and the physicians found Kamau, Rachael, and Talitha in Kamau's bedchamber, the stricken princess lying on the bed. The physicians examined Talitha and, as they had been commanded, shrugged their shoulders and otherwise registered confusion.

"We cannot tell what ails the princess," they lied, to the consternation of Prince Kamau and Princess Rachael. Minkah cleared his throat.

"Your highness," he said smoothly, "I know well that your desire is to be here with your guest. Still, someone should get word to the Princess Talitha's parents, and her brothers, of her illness. Perhaps we should dispatch a few of the warriors to relay the message and escort Princess Talitha's family here to watch with you until she recovers." Minkah knew that Kamau would want himself to lead the warriors to the Princess' kingdom, and Kamau did not disappoint his uncle.

"Yes, my desire is here, by Talitha's side," he said with wistfulness, "but I would be remiss in my duty if I allowed any but myself to lead warriors to the princess' kingdom; her parents will want to speak with someone who has been with her. I will immediately prepare a convoy for the journey to the princess' kingdom." Kamau kissed Talitha's hands and was as good as his word: in two hours, he and the warriors were off.

In three hours, Minkah had sent Rachael, too, off on some pretext, (and suggested to her handmaidens a bath similar to Talitha's). Soon Talitha awakened—in a dark, damp imprisonment under the castle. A guard noted her first stirrings, and after commissioning another to take his place, he took the news of the princess' awakening to Minkah. Kamau's uncle immediately descended to the holding place where he had sent Talitha.

"I suppose you are wondering why you are here, although you are obviously too proud to even deign to ask," said Minkah Chafulumisa. When Talitha did not answer, he spoke on as if she had: "I know who you are. I know your plans to destroy this house. And although Kamau is too young and besotted to do what needs to be done, or even to know what needs to be done, I have not been beguiled by your witchery. In the forest, even as I speak, trained hunters seek your brothers, whose enchantment has defiled the image of the sacred ibis. The hunters will kill every one of them. You--I will personally see to it --you will be burned as a sacrifice to the just God of our fathers at sunrise --as befits a witch." Minkah waited to hear the girl plead and weep. But he was disappointed. In respect, Minkah responded to her solemn silence: "I can tell you have a great deal of royal blood, although I never believed you were a princess." He turned and left Talitha alone with her thoughts.

Talitha could have screamed, tearing her hair and her clothes with confusion and frustration. But she had noticed that whoever had put her in the dungeon had also put her bag of needle weed and all the cloaks she had made in the dungeon as well. So she set to work. She could not allow herself to worry about her brothers (at least not any more than she had already worried); instead, as her fingers, automatically by now, began to fashion another cloak, Talitha silently prayed in her spirit for the safety of her brothers. *Hide them, Great Father,* she thought, *from the eyes of the hunters--at least until they are men again and can defend themselves. And, oh, God!* she wailed inwardly, *where is my Abayomi?* Tears blurred Talitha's eyes for a moment, but only a moment. She wouldn't be able to see if she let herself weep; she wouldn't be able to make cloaks if she couldn't see; so she simply aligned her inner forces with the demands of her duty. And she waited for daybreak.

On his way to the kingdom of Talitha's family, Kamau prayed, too. "Oh, God, keep Talitha whole until I, her parents and her brothers--her *brothers*!" He stopped mid sentence, suddenly remembering something. His uncle had said, "Get word to Talitha's parents, and *her brothers* . . . ." Kamau sharply reined in Montsho, to the confusion of his escort. *One assumes,* he thought, *that a person has parents, but does one assume that she has brothers--without asking anyone?* He could not recall an instance when Minkah and Talitha might have been alone to discuss such a matter, but even if they had, Talitha had not spoken to anyone, about anything, since she had come home with him. Kamau knew that he himself had not spoken to anyone of Talitha's brothers. Not anyone. When he had come home the last time, all he could think about was Talitha –her eyes, her mouth, how his heart had quickened when she had embraced him just before he had ridden home. Not a very talkative man, Kamau had mentioned meeting "a beautiful princess on a quest in the wood", but he had, to his shame, forgotten to mention her brothers. So how did his uncle know? Suddenly, Kamau felt troubled, not understanding at all why.

"We must return home," he said. Without a question, his convoy obeyed, turning their horses.

Back at Castle Obsidian, the sun was just clearing the horizon. The guards marched to Talitha's cell and roughly snatched her awake from a deep, long awaited sleep. Minkah, looking on, said, "Hurry! I want fires to be lit well before the sun is too high." Talitha, from force of habit, reached for her sack. One guard raised his arm to strike the bag from her grasp, but Minkah, laughing, stayed his hand.

"Her evil arts," he sneered, "can harm no one who has seen through them. Let her have her trash!" Talitha was allowed to take her needle-grass shirts to the courtyard, although her wrists were bound. A guard lifted her up to the bier, which already had wood underneath it ready for a fire. As the guard was leaving, Talitha wordlessly caught his eye, reaching out her hands. It was plain that she wanted to be untied. Knowing that the young woman would not be able to escape the bier without help, knowing that the girl had only ninety minutes, if that, to live, the guard looked into her eyes, shrugged, and loosed her wrists from the ropes. Talitha pulled her bag to her lap, but sat quietly, waiting.

Meanwhile, Minkah had reached the center of the courtyard, which had quickly filled with spectators. He paced and prayed while the guards coaxed the fire, stubborn because of the dew that hadn't had a chance to evaporate. As the fire finally caught and began to devour the wood, Minkah was lifting his hand for the attention of the crowd. He wanted to make a stirring speech. But something else had caught everyone's attention.

Riding with furious speed, Kamau and his convoy appeared in the courtyard. As they reined in their rearing and snorting horses, Minkah, furious himself, demanded, "What is the meaning of this? Nephew, you were to inform this woman's family--"

"I might well ask you the same question, Uncle," Kamau interrupted in a low, barely controlled voice. "'This woman,' as you so rudely call her, is a guest of our house and become my kinswoman. What means this fire? Extinguish it!" Kamau beckoned to his uncle's henchmen. After a moment's almost imperceptible indecision, they complied.

Minkah swallowed his fury and replied quietly to his nephew: "I will forbear the accomplishment of my duty long enough to explain. But I cannot allow your ignorance to become the downfall of this house. You should know that at your birth, there was a prophecy--"

"I already know of this prophecy. It is a matter of record. When I was of age, my father the king required that I read and understand it--or as much of it as he could understand, in the way that he understood it." At the word "prophecy," Talitha stopped rubbing the circulation back into her legs, which had gone to sleep as she knelt on the bier, watching the skies.

"What do you mean, 'in the way that he understood it'? Do you question your father's interpretation of the prophecy?" Minkah's voice rose a little in volume with this question.

"The prophecy, as I recall, states that after the appearance of the woman with the star, my reign 'will never be the same,'" Kamau patiently explained. "I think that my father's interpretation was precipitous and narrow. There are any manner of ways in which a reign can be changed."

"And what about the twelve ibis? Are there 'any number of ways' men warriors can be changed? Is there any doubt in your mind that this woman is a sorceress whose evil purposes remain hidden to us?" Minkah's voice had now risen so that all of the spectators could hear.

"Of course there is doubt, and more than doubt. She is a stranger to you. But I know Princess Talitha as well as I know myself," responded Kamau. He looked at Talitha, now sitting up on the bier, reaching for her sack. "While there may be evil in her circumstance, there is no evil in her purpose or in herself."
"You are a bewitched, besotted young fool!" Minkah was saying with anger and sorrow, when their argument was interrupted by a sound of wonder from the crowd. Minkah and Kamau looked up. From the lake behind the courtyard flew twelve iridescent black and white ibis, safe and unharmed. Talitha sobbed with joy and began to pull cloaks from her sack. The birds flew straight for her,

one by one, and as each of the twelve reached Talitha, she stretched up and draped one cloak about each of the sinuous necks. After receiving a cloak, each bird lit upon the ground--and became a man. So Jabari, Jawhar, Chinelo, Harith, Akil, Liu, Nizam, Fadil, Chijoke, Masomakali, Shawki and Adisa regained their original states as Talitha's beloved brothers.

"Seize them!" shouted Minkah. "Destroy them!" But as Minkah's men moved to obey, Jawhar spoke.

"Is it the custom in this kingdom to punish where there is no crime? To defend where there has been no attack? In my father's kingdom, even a proven criminal is given a chance to speak in his own defense."

"Hold!" said Kamau. "Talitha's brother is right. Although I have an idea of how the story goes myself, you, uncle, you need to hear." And alighting from Montsho, Kamau strode over to the bier, reached up for Talitha and swung her down.

"Now I may speak," said Talitha, and told the story of her brothers from beginning to end. Everyone in the courtyard hung on her every word. (And as she spoke, far away in the wood near her brothers' cabin, unknown to anyone but God at the time, violets bloomed--but more than twelve this time: this time, scores of violets carpeted the wood with fragrance and color.)

At the end of Talitha's story, Minkah Chafulumisa fell to one knee and pressed his forehead to one of the Princess' ruined hands. "I beg forgiveness, Highness, although I deserve to take your place on that bier. Only speak, and I willingly offer my body to the flames."

"Rise to your feet, Minkah Chafulumisa," replied Talitha. Tears stood in her eyes. "A kingdom could ask for no guardian more faithful than you."

"Yes, Uncle," echoed Kamau. "Facing what you thought was a powerful evil, facing accusations of rebellion and treason,

you valued the kingdom more than your safety. You took your life in your hands to keep a promise you made to my father the King. He is dead, but your word lives, and that is the mark of a man of integrity and honor. Still," Kamau added sternly, "You should not have hidden your heart from me--however bewitched you believed I was."

"And never again will I, Majesty," replied Minkah, his eyes shining also with unshed tears. "Today, I see your father in you. With joy I quit my position as your guardian. I realize that the house of Kamau is in good hands." And he knelt again--to his King. "Long live the King," Minkah cried, and the people echoed his cry.

"I hope," said Kamau, who felt full of emotion as well, "that you will stay on as my closest advisor. You have proven yourself worthy." Then Kamau turned to Talitha. "Dearest lady," he was beginning, when Talitha sank to her knees, nearly fainting with exhaustion. Kamau ran to her side and carried her to his uncle's chambers. "Dearest lady," he quickly changed his speech, "now is the time for some much needed rest." The waiting women again bathed and ministered to Talitha, finally leaving her to rest in Minkah's bed.

Princess Talitha slept for twenty hours. She opened her eyes to behold the face of Kamau, who had been looking in on her, off and on (along with her twelve brothers) while she had slept.

"Abayomi," she whispered.

"It's good to hear my name in your mouth again, Talitha," he answered. "How do you feel?"

"Much better. For a long time, I have felt so heavily burdened, so guilty, so alone--"

"I was here."

"You were," Talitha agreed, and touched his cheek. "But you were not as close as I wanted you to be. I couldn't explain to you. I felt that you were trying to understand me, that you were committed to help me, that I could depend on you, but I felt you were giving me so much, when --when I could give you so little."

"But I understood." Kamau stopped Talitha from interrupting by touching her lips. "I don't know how I understood. I don't know why I was not frightened or driven away by what you were doing. I only knew that you were a good woman-- remember, I had met some of your brothers and that a good woman only works to *un*do evil, not create it. You were beautiful and good and courageous, and I wanted to be a part of your life. I wanted to help you."

"God sent you to us," Talitha said fervently. "God sent you."

"God sent us to each other," Kamau corrected her. "So it seems only fitting--I wanted to wait until your father –until your parents--Talitha, suddenly, I can't say what I want to say."

"Then say what you can."

"I've loved you since you came out from behind that tree. When I saw your tears of joy, I felt it was my joy, too. When you wept in sorrow, I felt my heart breaking. Now-- I feel like a dog to say it --your sorrow is over, and my heart is breaking again: you'll be leaving me. You don't need me any more."

"I don't need you, but I love you, Abayomi. How could you not know?"

"Then will you have me as your husband?"

"When my parents come, I'll tell them that I will have no other man." Kamau's face lit up from within.

"Everyone knows that *he* will have no other woman," said Rachael, who was coming in. "My brother, you must leave now. This visit is on the verge of becoming very improper."

"I don't see why I can't stay, now that you are here, to keep things proper," Kamau protested.

"Well . . . for a little longer, then. But when *I* leave, *you* leave."

"You don't make a very impressive chaperone, Rachael," said Talitha.

"You're saying I should call Umm?" At Kamau and Talitha's expressions, Rachael burst out laughing. "Oh," she sighed then, "I'm so ashamed I missed all the excitement!"

"Everyone knows it wasn't your fault, Rachael," reassured Talitha.

"And Uncle has apologized at least a thousand times since I woke up. The women believe they'll all be exiled! Now, brother, release the princess' hand!"

"I wonder if they'll ever be whole again," sighed Talitha.

"They'll always be the most beautiful hands in the world to me," said Kamau. "And I know your brothers would say the same."

When King Abdu and Queen Rukiya finally arrived, they were very charmed by Prince Kamau, and awed by his, Talitha's, and their sons' adventures. But Abdu, Talitha and her brothers were most surprised by Queen Rukiya's revelation.

"I blame myself for your trouble," she whispered.

"But how can you--?" began Abdu, when the queen interrupted.

"Let me tell you. Remember long ago, when I was carrying Adisa, Moyo, told us that I was carrying my twelfth son? Remember how disappointed I was?"

"I remember I made some thoughtless remark, and you ran off somewhere," said the king. The queen related her story to the young people.

"You did all of that, expecting a *baby*?" interrupted Rachael. "You two" –indicating Rukiya and Talitha—"must be the sturdiest women I know!" The queen laughed.

"Well, Adisa wasn't due for months yet. Just because a woman is expecting, it doesn't mean that she's disabled!" Rukiya looked at her daughter and Rachael. "I want you to remember that," she said, to the distraction of them both. "I suppose," she continued her story, "that violet drank some of my tears that day. It was fate that you would pick those violets, Talitha."

"So you think it was your fault —that 'ridiculous fate' you and Father told me of?" Talitha asked.

"I don't know. I don't know." Rukiya covered her face and shook her head.

"And I don't know how my brothers were linked to that plant, Mother," said Talitha, "but I see now that my destiny was far from 'ridiculous.' What happened to me in that wood helped to deepen my spirit. It found me the man I love —a man I know now to be steadfast and wise. And—"

"And it bound us and our sister in love and trust. Your prayers were answered, Mother," added Adisa. His brothers looked at each other and nodded.

"And what man would give up the opportunity to know the ibis from the inside out?" asked Chinelo.

"Imagine the poetry I will write!" exulted Jawhar. All of Talitha's brothers could see, whether they said so or not, how going through their ordeal had richened their lives.

"It's plain that this experience has somehow been worthwhile for everyone involved —especially me," said Kamau. "But —if you will indulge me, your majesty —I must disagree with the King." The King raised a dark eyebrow.

"Disagree? With what?" he asked.

"That a daughter —simply because she is the thirteenth heir—cannot gain a kingdom. I think, your majesties, that if you can grant your blessing upon our —Talitha's and my—union, you will find you have *two* kingdoms."

"You are willing to give up your own for the hand of my daughter?" King Abdu asked facetiously. "Notice, my dear," he added to Queen Rukiya, "they aren't asking for our *consent*."

"Did you notice her asking our consent to this quest?" exclaimed Rukiya.

"And, Father, Mother, I tell you now, but with love, honor and respect—"

"Well?" came from the King, whose eyes were sparkling with mirth.

"—that I have chosen this man, Kamau," finished Talitha. "I could choose no other."

"I can see that you have talked this young man into going along with your choice," said the Queen.

"Oh, please!" interrupted Rachael, laughing. "Do you really think she had to do much persuading?"

"My own heart persuaded me, your majesties, once I looked upon the face of your daughter," said Kamau. "Please, majesties, grant us your blessing." Abdu squeezed the hand of his wife. She met his eyes and nodded solemnly.

"It pleases us," Abdu said. "May heaven bless your union – with fourteen daughters!"

The union of Kamau and Talitha was the birth of one great kingdom, for King Abdu, his first son, Chinelo, and Kamau, agreed to unite the houses of Abdu and Kamau. The Kingdom of Abdu-Kamau became great and full of power in many ways, and their enemies could find no means to overthrow it. All over the world this kingdom became renowned for its wisdom, might, and integrity. And Kamau and Talitha lived in joy to the end of their days, raising seven sons and seven daughters in the nurture and admonition of the great God who formed all things.

~ The End ~

[1](#) His name means "worshipper of God."

[2](#) Her name means "she rises on high."

[3](#) Their names mean, respectively, "thought of God;" "one who reasons;" "voice;" "arranger;" "generous;" "God gives talent;" "sharp eyes;" "cultivator;" "historian;" "jewel;" and "yearning for right conduct."

[4](#) His name means "good health."

[5](#) His name means "one who makes his meaning clear."

[6](#) *His* name means "the king's word."

[7](#) His name means "quiet warrior."

[8](#) This name means "born to bring me joy."

[9](#) The horse's name means "black."

[10](#) His name means "swift justice."

[11](#) Her name means "mother."

[12](#) Her name means "ewe."

ABOUT THE AUTHOR

J. Regina Blackwell is a zaftig, black, Christian, voracious reader and movie-watcher from Virginia. She has two beautiful daughters and two dogs, both mutts. She spends most of her time at home, in the classroom/office, in the theatres, in the video/book stores, in libraries, with friends and other family, and arguing with near strangers on the Internet.

ABOUT THE ILLUSTRATOR

Steve A. Prince, a native of New Orleans, Louisiana, and residing in Meadville, Pennsylvania, is an educator who has taught privately, middle school, college, and is currently an Artist in Residence at Allegheny College. Having received his BFA from Xavier University of Louisiana and his MFA from Michigan State University, Prince has shown his faith-based art in various solo, group, and juried exhibitions in America, the Bahamas, and Brazil, to name only a few locations. He is married to the writer Valerie Sweeney Prince; they have three children: two artists, Imani and Elijah, in college, and a community organizer, Etienne, in elementary school.

www.ingramcontent.com/pod-product-compliance
Lightning Source LLC
Chambersburg PA
CBHW031436040426
42444CB00006B/835